WATER

EARTH'S BIOMES

WATER

TOM WARHOL

 **Marshall Cavendish**
Benchmark
New York

To my mother and father, for their encouragement and support,
and to Lisa, for helping my talents to show through.

Marshall Cavendish Benchmark
99 White Plains Road
Tarrytown, New York 10591-9001
www.marshallcavendish.us

All Web sites were available and accurate when this book was sent to press.

Editor: Karen Ang
Editorial Director: Michelle Bisson
Art Director: Anahid Hamparian
Series Designer: Patrice Sheridan

Library of Congress Cataloging-in-Publication Data

Warhol, Tom.
Water / by Tom Warhol.
p. cm. — (Earth's biomes)
Summary: "Explores water biomes and covers where they are located as well
as the plants and animals that inhabit them"—Provided by publisher.
Includes bibliographical references and index.
ISBN-13: 978-0-7614-2192-4
ISBN-10: 0-7614-2192-0
1. Aquatic ecology—Juvenile literature. 2. Water—Juvenile literature.
I. Title. II. Series.

QH541.5.W3W37 2006
577.6—dc22

2006011979

Front cover caption: A coral reef
Title page: A sea anemone and sea cucumber
Back cover: A Galapagos sea lion
Photo research by Candlepants, Inc.

Photo Researchers Inc.: Andrew J. Martinez, 3, 47; Peter Scoones, 8; Science Photo Library, 18; Jeffery Greenberg,
21(left); Ray Coleman, 21(right); A.N.T., 23; Tom McHugh, 52; NASA, 55; Michael P. Gadomski, 66. *Minden
Pictures:* Fred Bavendam, 10, 31; Tui De Roy, 14, 38, 53, back cover; Flip Nicklin, 16, 43, 45, 74; D.P.
Wilson,/FLPA, 22; Frans Lanting, 25, 36, 56, 73; Chris Newbert, 26, 44; Norbert Wu, 28, 33; Jim Brandenburg,
37; Mike Parry, 42; Tim Fitzharris, 48, 71; Reg Morrison/Auscape, 57; Michael Durham, 59; Yva Momatuik/John
Eastcott, 68; Rob Reijnen/Foto Natura, 69; Gerry Ellis, 70. *Tom Warhol:* 7, 40, 51, 54. *Corbis:* Craig Tuttle, 13;
David Muench, 64; Tom Van Sant, 65. *Animals Animals/Earth Scenes:* Stephen Dalton, 58; Jeff Bergdoll, 62.
Printed in China
1 3 5 6 4 2

CONTENTS

INTRODUCTION

WATER: THE BASIS OF LIFE

The last place one expects to find water may be in the dry leaf litter and dead wood of the forest floor on a mountainside. But in a narrow cleft where rock has been exposed, a trickle of water begins, slowly leaking out of a reservoir built up by rains and snowmelt beneath the mountain rock. Flowing down with the slope, the water picks up speed, carrying leaves, sticks, and small creatures along with it. The water's speed creates so much force that it begins to dig into the earth and carry soil in its swelling liquid mass. The soil gives even greater weight to the flow and allows the water to travel faster and widen its own channel. The flow uncovers rocks, which split the stream into channels as the water continues to seek its downward course. Some of these individual channels may join together, forming one larger channel again. Others may split off, carving their own routes down the mountain. All these channels will eventually reach the same place in the valley at the base of the mountain.

Once these and other streams that drain the rain and groundwater from the high ground meet in the valley, the stream becomes a river. Its size and increased flow are able to carry large debris. The river makes its way down the valley, carrying large debris in its increased flow. The channel it travels in was carved by the river itself over millions of years.

The water eventually reaches more level ground away from the steep terrain of the mountains and hills. The river widens and flattens. The water then passes farms that line its banks. It carries materials that provide sustenance for the various life-forms that live along the river's course. The number of fish and other animal life increases here. Trout rest in quiet pools sheltered from the main flow of the river, and caddis fly nymphs feed on floating plant and animal matter.

As the river nears the sea, its waters take on salt. Many freshwater plants and animals can't live in the salt water, so more salt-tolerant plant communities take root. The water slows, releasing its load of sediment, creating mud flats. Millions of fish and birds feed and breed in this rich habitat.

Much of the sediments—sand, silt, and clay—and plant and animal matter carried downstream end up in the ocean. There they nourish many sea creatures.

This movement of water from high mountains to the sea's depths has created the landscape of the planet today and provided a nursery for all life on Earth. Every living thing is dependent on water. The origins of all life are, in fact, the water itself.

Streams that begin in hilly or mountainous areas often form waterfalls where they flow over exposed rock, such as this small waterfall in western Massachusetts.

7

These underwater stromatolites display the life processes of cyanobacteria over thousands of years. Cyanobacteria were some of the first organisms to live in the Earth's waters.

1

HOW WATER SHAPES THE WORLD

A precise set of conditions allowed the first organism to appear in the Earth's earliest seas nearly 4 billion years ago. More than 70 percent of the Earth's surface was covered with water, and its distance from the Sun provided the ideal temperatures for life to grow and breed in this liquid nursery. No other planet in the solar system has so much water.

THE BEGINNING

The Earth's oceans began to form about 4 billion years ago, as the planet was cooling after its fiery, volcanic formation. The raw rock that composed the Earth divided into two types. The heavier rock sank in toward the mantle, one of the Earth's inner layers. The sinking rock created deep basins that later became the ocean floors, called the oceanic crust. The lighter materials rose and formed the planet's continental crust, or land masses.

As the molten Earth cooled, the water vapor that was spewed into the air by all the volcanic activity condensed and began to fall as rain.

By about 3.8 billion years ago rainwater that carved river channels on the land masses and melting ice comets that fell from space supplied the water that gradually formed the planet's oceans. Scientists believe that every living thing on Earth evolved from the first creatures in the newly formed oceans. However, early evolution was an extremely slow process. These single-celled organisms floated alone in the oceans for 1.6 billion years before conditions were right for them to begin to evolve into new life-forms. These new creatures were tiny and produced their own food by photosynthesizing, or turning sunlight and water into sugars for energy. Oxygen, which is a byproduct of this process, filled the atmosphere and allowed new life-forms to evolve and colonize both sea and land.

All the chemical compounds and processes that are necessary for life as we know it can be found in water. Every single life-form relies on water for survival. In fact, most life-forms are made up of an average of

Moon jellyfish, which can be found in both the Pacific and Atlantic oceans, may grow to be nearly 16 inches in diameter and are mostly made up of water.

65 percent water. Aquatic organisms are about 80 percent water, but some, like jellyfish, can be 95 percent water.

THE WATER CYCLE

Many animals on Earth cannot drink salt water or live in it, so it's surprising that the oceans are the main source of fresh water for all land organisms. This is even more impressive when considering that for every 1 pound (0.45 kilograms) of growth, a plant needs 100 pounds (45 kg) of water.

The world's supply of water is not limitless, although it may seem so. Fortunately, the planet has evolved a circulation system that reuses the same water over and over again. Water that falls as rain or snow, called precipitation, has been around the world countless times before.

Oceans absorb warmth from the sun and air during the day and release the heat slowly at night. More heat is absorbed in summer, and more is lost in winter. As the ocean heats up, some water evaporates from its surface. This water vapor is lifted by rising warm air. When it comes into contact with the cooler air in the upper atmosphere, the water vapor condenses around tiny particles—such as dust, pollen grains from plants, or even particulates from pollution—and forms clouds. These clouds are then moved around the planet by winds. When the clouds become large and the water is too heavy to stay suspended, it falls to the Earth again as rain, snow, hail, or sleet.

As this precipitation falls onto land, most of it seeps through the soil into aquifers and other underground cavities. This unseen water accounts for about 30 percent of the water in rivers and lakes. Once the soil becomes saturated, there isn't any more room for the rainwater. The rain then flows over the ground and collects in lakes or continues downstream into rivers. Much of it eventually makes its way to the ocean again, completing the cycle. Ninety-eight percent of all the water on Earth is contained in the five large ocean basins: the Pacific, Atlantic, Indian, Southern, and Arctic oceans. The remaining 2 percent is made up of fresh water from many sources. Most of that—75 percent—is held in glaciers, and the rest is in lakes, ponds, streams, and rivers.

SHAPING THE WORLD

Millions of years of weathering—the process of breaking down a structure's composition through the mechanical and chemical action of weather—can reduce the size of landforms such as mountains. For example, the Appalachian Mountains in the eastern United States are a much older mountain range than the Rocky Mountains in the West. The Appalachians are much smaller now, but when they were young landforms, they were just as big as the Rockies.

The slightly acidic quality of water makes it capable of breaking down rock. Certain types of rock are fairly resistant to the weathering process. The clear water that flows over these rocks is called soft water because it contains few minerals. The cloudy water that flows over soft, sedimentary rocks is full of minerals and is called hard water.

The sediments released by weathering are carried by streams and rivers out to the edge of continents and deposited in the ocean, adding to continental shelves. These wide collections of sediments give many continents a shallow coastline that extends about 40 miles (65 km) out to sea. Although they only account for 8 percent of oceans, continental shelves contain the majority of Earth's marine life. The constantly deposited sediments create varied shallow-water habitats.

The rock beneath the water is every bit as varied as landforms are on the continents. In fact, some of the mountains beneath the sea, such as the

The world's coastlines have been shaped by millions of years of natural change. Here, starfish cling to rocks on a sandy beach on Oregon's Pacific coast.

Azore Islands in the North Atlantic, are taller than any mountains on land. The Marianas Trench off the west coast of South America is, at 7 miles (11 km) deep, the deepest rift valley in the world and the deepest part of all the oceans.

Today the Earth is made up of thirteen major plates of rock that float on a mantle of liquid, partly molten rock. These plates have broken apart, come together, and moved around the planet over geological history, forming the continents and ocean basins. Where some of these plates meet, volcanic activity occurs. The largest geological features on Earth are the mid-ocean ridges. They rise from the seafloor to heights of nearly 2

Calderas—or volcanic craters—collect water and develop aquatic communities. This caldera lake formed on the Cerro Azul volcano in the Galapagos Islands.

miles (3 km) and stretch for 27,963 miles (45,000 km) around the world.

The ridges lie beneath the Atlantic, Indian, and Pacific oceans. The continuing volcanic activity that helps to vent the heat under Earth's mantle is released along the ridges, among other places. The magma, or molten rock, that spews out continuously creates new seafloor as it cools, pushing the oceanic plates apart. Mountains are also created along the ridge as magma builds up over time. The Hawaiian Islands and the Galapagos Islands are the tops of volcanoes originating from the Pacific mid-ocean ridge.

Water has also shaped the world through its solid state. During the Ice Ages, when glaciers covered parts of the Earth, sheets of ice thousands of feet thick advanced and retreated over the landscape in response to temperature changes. These massive glaciers ground down bedrock while picking up and carrying soils, boulders, and any other debris in their way. As the glaciers melted, they dropped the debris hundreds of miles from its point of origin. The glaciers destroyed old landforms and created new ones, like elongated hills, ridges, and flat plains.

AQUATIC ENVIRONMENTS

From the first single-celled organism floating alone in the early seas to the amazing variety of life found in oceans, lakes, and rivers today has been a long journey. Over 230,000 species of marine life have been discovered. Because only a tiny fraction of the world's oceans have been explored, scientists estimate that anywhere between 1 and 100 million species are left to be discovered.

While some of the species in different freshwater environments are similar, most aquatic environments have their own distinctive and diverse biota. The most obvious distinction is between fresh and salt water. Virtually no organisms that live in fresh water can tolerate salt water, and vice-versa. Notable exceptions are anadromous fish species, like salmon, which migrate from salt water into the far reaches of freshwater rivers in order to spawn, or breed. Catadromous fish like eels migrate from fresh water to salt water for the same purpose.

However, the aquatic world is not black and white. There are variations between these two extremes. Estuaries are areas of brackish water—a mix of salt and fresh water—and are the result of the tides that wash into the mouths of rivers. This constantly shifting mix of salt water and fresh water creates nurseries—protected places for eggs to hatch and young to mature—for millions of fish and shellfish.

Within freshwater habitats, there are distinct differences between flowing water and standing water environments. Some species can exist in both habitats, but many others are specific to one or the other.

A giant kelp forest and coral in California's Channel Islands National Park.

2

OCEANS

There is a lot of water in the oceans. This may sound like an overly simple statement, but it is a first step to understanding that the Earth is very much a water world. For land creatures like humans, this may be hard to understand. Humans may be dependent on oceans, but people, of course, do not and cannot live in water—most have never even been in a boat out in the deep sea.

OCEAN CIRCULATION

The ocean winds that have guided sea travel for thousands of years are produced by oceans after they absorb heat from the Sun. Tropical waters absorb the most heat. As they release it, the hot air rises and cool air rushes in to replace it, creating winds. All this moving air affects the ocean currents. The currents move at a 45-degree angle to the wind direction because the winds are affected by the rotation of the Earth. This rotation causes the winds to move to the right in the Northern Hemisphere and to the left in the Southern Hemisphere.

For example, the winds in the North Atlantic Ocean move west from Europe toward the Caribbean Sea, then they curve northward as they become deflected by the North American continent. This circulation of wind and surface water travels more slowly back east toward north Europe. The whole cycle is called the Northern Atlantic Gyre. It is kept circulating by the shape of the land masses in the North Atlantic Ocean. There are two gyres in each of the Pacific, Atlantic, and Indian oceans.

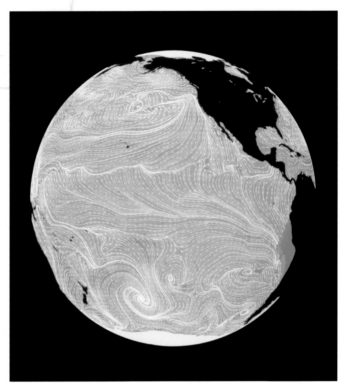

A satellite map shows wind speed and direction over parts of the Pacific Ocean. Blue arrows indicate wind speeds of 0 to 8 miles per hour; purple and pink represent speeds of 9 to 26 miles per hour; and red and orange arrows show speeds of 27 to 45 miles per hour.

The effect is less in the Southern Hemisphere because there are fewer land masses to deflect the currents. The Antarctic Circumpolar Current, an east-west flow of cold air through the Southern Ocean, also lessens the circular movement of the southern gyres. Winds along the equator move parallel to the equator because the rotation of the Earth has less effect there.

The Oceans of the World

For many years only four oceans were officially recognized by many scientists and other people around the world: the Atlantic, Pacific, Arctic, and Indian oceans. But in 2000, the International Hydrographic Organization defined the borders of a fifth ocean, the Southern Ocean. This ocean completely surrounds Antarctica and stretches from the continent's coast to 60 degrees south latitude. In the past, the Southern Ocean was referred to as the Antarctic Ocean but was merely considered to be a portion of the Atlantic, Indian, and Pacific oceans.

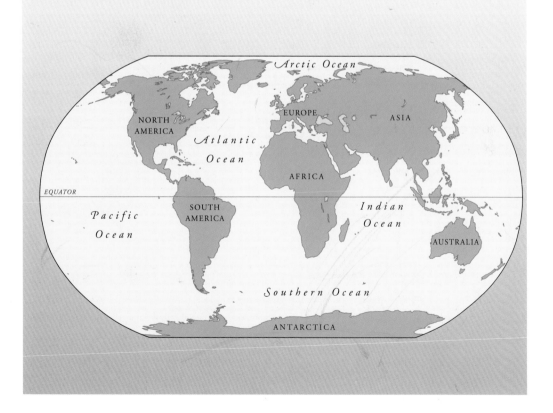

CLIMATE CONTROL

The movement of gyres is not only good for ocean travel. It also keeps the waters circulating, which is vital for marine life. As polar seawater becomes cold and dense, it sinks below the surface. The gyres replace this cold water with warm surface water from the tropics, which helps to moderate the cold temperatures of the polar seas. The cold water—some of which has not reached the surface for centuries—eventually mixes with warm water. This mixing allows nutrients held in deep waters to be brought to the surface for phytoplankton and other organisms to feed upon.

The most important thing that oceans do for the planet, though, is to control and moderate Earth's climate. These salty waters keep the planet from heating up or cooling down too much by storing heat and moving it around the world. Because oceans absorb and release heat more slowly than land does, temperatures of coastal lands are milder than temperatures of inland areas. Without the oceans, the air over land would be intolerably hot in the daytime and terribly cold at night.

The other great service oceans perform for the global climate is to act as a giant carbon dioxide store, or reservoir. The oceans absorb atmospheric carbon dioxide and hold it, preventing it from filling up the atmosphere and raising global temperatures.

TIDES

Movement of ocean waters is not only influenced by the winds, it is also affected by heavenly bodies in our solar system. The gravitational pull of the Moon as it orbits Earth has a daily effect on oceans. The water on whichever side of Earth is closest to the Moon gets pulled toward the Moon. This causes the daily high tides in most parts of the world. The sides not facing the Moon are compressed because of centrifugal force—a force exerted by the rotation of Earth—causing low tides.

Low tide (left) and high tide (right) at Hopewell Rocks in New Brunswick, in Canada's Bay of Fundy. This bay has the world's highest tides.

The Sun, while much farther away from Earth than the Moon, also has a gravitational influence on tides. When the Sun is either on the opposite side of Earth from the Moon (during a full moon) or on the same side (during a new moon), the gravitational effect on tides is doubled. These twice-monthly high tides are called spring tides. When the moon is at right angles to the Sun and Earth (during the half-moons), very low tides, called neap tides, occur.

CHAIN OF LIFE

Because of all these changing tides, winds, and circulation of warm and cold waters, this liquid world contains an astonishing variety of life, from the largest creature on the planet—the blue whale—to some of the smallest, such as plankton.

Just as photosynthesis is the key to all life on land, so it is in the oceans as well. Phytoplankton are tiny microscopic plants that create their own food by converting the oceans' large supply of carbon dioxide into carbohydrates (simple sugars) by means of photosynthesis. The byproduct of photosynthesis is oxygen, necessary for all life on the planet.

While many people are familiar with the role of land plants in photosynthesis and storing carbon, most have no idea that these tiny phytoplankton produce half of all the oxygen in the world. The sugars they produce are utilized by other life-forms when they eat the phytoplankton. The byproduct of this consumption and these creatures' other life processes is carbon dioxide, which is released into the water or air and eventually reabsorbed by plants. The live phytoplankton that are not eaten by other organisms eventually die and fall to the bottom of the ocean. They are either eaten along the way by creatures dwelling in lower zones or they settle onto the ocean floor, where bacteria turn them back into carbon dioxide. When ocean waters mix in the spring or during storms, phytoplankton can reproduce in great numbers because

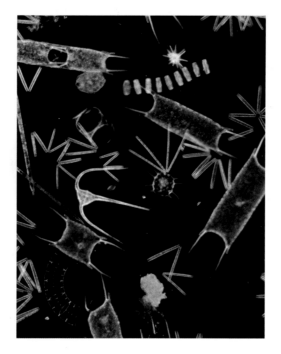

there is a wealth of nutrients for them to eat. This bloom of life is the basis for the whole ocean food chain. It ensures that there is more than enough phytoplankton to feed the zooplankton, which are a type of single-celled and multicellular animal life in the ocean. In turn, the zooplankton are eaten by fish. These fish are then consumed by

Microscopic plants in phytoplankton provide food for countless organisms and oxygen for much of world. Phytoplankton floating in the oceans may also include microscope organisms called diatoms and dinoflagellates.

larger predators, such as big fish and whales. The chain continues as other organisms feed on the whales and large fish. If the phytoplankton reproduced more gradually, their entire population might be eaten by the zooplankton and the whole food chain would collapse.

Links in the Food Chain

The food chain in the ocean usually starts with the plankton being eaten by fish and other small creatures, followed by larger animals eating those fish. The chain continues on to include large ocean animals like whales and sharks. But sometimes a link or two in this chain is skipped, and larger ocean creatures will eat the very tiny ones at the beginning of the food chain. There are eleven species of whales that feed on plankton and very small fish. These species include blue whales and whale sharks. These marine animals have long, flexible plates called baleen in their mouths. The baleen is covered in bristles and filters small food from the water.

A whale shark swims with a wide-open mouth, ready to catch and filter plankton from the water.

CLIMATIC ZONES

As with land habitats, ocean waters are not all the same. Land plants and the animals that depend on them are restricted to specific habitats by a number of factors, including geology and soil type. Ocean life also only exists where each particular species is best adapted. Possibly the most important factor influencing all life on Earth is climate. From the poles to the tropics, temperature, amount of sunlight, precipitation, and wind govern what can grow or live in any given region. Temperature variations between the different regions of the world have a dramatic effect on the world's oceans, which can be divided into three distinct zones: tropical, temperate, and polar.

Tropical Oceans

Tropical seas occur on both sides of the equator in a belt around the planet. They provide the warm water that is circulated throughout all the oceans, balancing the frigid temperatures in the polar seas and helping maintain life there. Since terrestrial—land—environments in the tropics are some of the richest and most diverse land-based systems on Earth, it is surprising that tropical oceans are some of the least productive of all the oceans. Despite warm temperatures and plenty of sunlight, tropical seas only produce one-quarter the amount of life-forms of temperate oceans. The open water of the tropics may not be full of life, but where the waters meet land, life abounds. This region is where coral reefs, mangrove forests, and seagrass beds exist and thrive.

Coral Reefs While coral reefs can grow in a variety of places, the conditions in the tropics are especially suited to their formation: warm temperatures between 64 and 86 degrees Fahrenheit (18 and 30 degrees Celsius) and clear, sunlit waters. Because they need bright sunlight, reefs usually form in shallow waters just offshore of islands or other

An aerial view of a barrier reef around Mount Otamanu in Tahiti.

land masses. These rich habitats provide shelter and food for a wide variety of fish, sponges, anemones, algae, and many other creatures. The Great Barrier Reef, off the northeastern coast of Australia, is actually made up of 2,100 different reefs and stretches for 1,429 miles (2,300 km).

All reefs have the same basic shape: a long ridge with a flat top, a sloping landward edge, and a more abrupt seaward face. The reef flat is the uppermost and shallowest part, and corals grow horizontally there because they need to stay submerged. The diversity is low on this part of the reef because of the warmer temperatures.

On the landward side, a calm, sandy-bottomed lagoon usually forms because the reef breaks the waves coming toward shore. On the seaward side, the edge is formed by boulders tossed in by the waves and held in place by red algae. The reef slope below this edge is the most diverse part of the coral reef.

Corals and Reef Formation

Corals are part of a larger group of animals called Cnidarians, which includes other sea life such as jellyfish and sea anemones. An individual coral polyp is a very simple creature, shaped sort of like a tube with a central mouth and surrounding tentacles that take in food. Hard corals live colonially, numbering in the thousands or even millions, creating their own limestone "skeletons," which build up on the seafloor and anchor them. As the corals eat, they also take in seawater, which is filled with dissolved calcium carbonate. Corals do not use the calcium carbonate for nutrition, they secrete it. It then settles beneath them. When an entire colony of corals does this, over time it creates a ridge, or coral reef, which supports them and other creatures. Each coral species creates its own type of skeleton in the shape of boulders, branches, or fans.

The hard corals are helped along in their growth by single-celled algae called zooxanthellae that live within the corals' tissues. The corals provide the algae with carbon dioxide for photosynthesis, and their bodies shelter the algae from predators. As the algae photosynthesize, the corals also can consume the sugars and oxygen they create. This symbiotic relationship gives the corals the added nutrition necessary to grow three times faster than normal, ensuring that reef formation outpaces reef erosion.

A coral reef teeming with life along the shores of the Solomon Islands in the Pacific.

Three types of reefs—fringing reefs, barrier reefs, and coral atolls—may form, depending upon the water temperature, the geology of the seabed, and the action of waves. Fringing reefs grow in shallow waters along a continental coast or island shore. They build up to sea level then grow out into the ocean. A barrier reef forms when a fringing reef continues to grow out toward the continental shelf and forms a lagoon between it and land.

When mountains form from underwater volcanic activity, they sometimes break the surface of the ocean. The warm, shallow waters around these islands create the ideal conditions for the formation of coral atolls. These reefs encircle the island, forming a lagoon that is connected to the ocean by channels, or gaps in the reef. Coral atolls can also surround sandy islands.

Reef erosion occurs naturally due to the action of waves and animals breaking the reef down into sand. Sponges and bivalve mollusks will actually bore into the reef to create safe hiding places. Parrotfish eat the hard coral, grinding it up and excreting sand.

If the reef erodes away, the sand may become an island called a coral cay that can then be colonized by land plants and animals. The sand created by erosion may also be added back to the reef and cemented to it by red algae. This will make the reef even stronger than it was before.

Mangrove Forests Mangroves are an example of an organism that can exist in brackish water. The many different species of these resilient tropical trees grow in dense, impenetrable thickets in estuaries. They are the centerpieces of ecosystems that provide important wildlife habitat and help protect coastlines from damaging storms and high waves. Arching roots called prop roots take in air above the muddy, oxygen-poor water or when they are exposed at low tide. The roots also serve to hold the soil in place, both on land and below the water.

Many creatures take advantage of the shelter the mangroves provide. Sea life such as oysters, mussels, barnacles, and anemones anchor themselves to the strong prop roots, while a wide variety of insects and spiders live among the aboveground branches and leaves. Birds nest in the branches as well. Grazing creatures like antelope and pigs roam beneath the mangroves. In some mangrove forests, predators such as mongooses, tigers, and otters hunt among them.

Because the seeds of mangroves are so nutrient-rich, they are a favorite food source for gypsid crabs, one of two species of crab that frequent mangrove forests worldwide. The crabs also feed on the mangrove roots. Because of this close association, gypsid crabs have a dramatic effect on the distribution of mangrove forests. If crab populations are high in one part of the swamp, the mangroves there will not be able to reproduce easily.

Sea grass grows alongside underwater mangrove roots in this mangrove forest in the western-Pacific island nation of Palau.

Sea Grass Beds Sea grasses are unusual among ocean plants because, like land plants, they produce flowers. Sea grass beds occur in shallow, sheltered ocean waters with sandy bottoms next to mangrove forests and coral reefs. Their extensive root systems grow quickly, holding the sandy soil in place, and their wide, flat leaves slow the waves. These adaptations, like the mangroves' prop roots, help prevent coastal erosion.

Sea grass beds also provide an ideal environment for many different organisms. Seahorses, shrimp, lobsters, and fish use the dense beds for shelter from predators, while turtles and dugongs, herbivorous sea mammals, feed on the leaves.

Temperate Oceans

The temperate oceans of the world stretch in bands between tropical and polar oceans in both the Northern and Southern Hemispheres. These are the most productive waters of all the oceans, full of nutrients and phytoplankton. In the midst of the spring bloom, there may be as many as 425 million individual phytoplankton in every square meter of water. They support very large populations of animals and plants. Copepods—tiny shrimp about 0.08 inches (2 mm) long—are the most numerous animals on the planet. However, the amount of ocean life varies throughout the year. Spring and summer temperatures encourage growth, while the cold temperatures and reduced sunlight of winters inhibit it.

The upper layers of temperate seas are strongly influenced by the seasonal climate. The warmth from the summer sun that makes life easier for so many creatures only extends about 160 feet (50 m) down into the water. The boundary between this warm layer of water and the cold layer below, the thermocline, serves as a barrier to small creatures and nutrients. Winter storms break up the thermocline, mixing nutrients throughout the water column. When temperatures in spring heat the water up enough, phytoplankton can "bloom," or reproduce in large numbers, and the seasonal, productive period begins again for temperate oceans.

One reason that most temperate seas are so rich is that river flow constantly dumps nutrients from land masses onto the continental shelf. In some areas, as in the Bay of Fundy, off Nova Scotia, the tidal action is so strong that there is constant mixing, resulting in abundant wildlife year-round. But many temperate ocean creatures spend the winter in deeper waters, moving little and using little energy, or they migrate to warmer waters.

Migrations

Because of the seasonal availability of food in temperate seas, many animals have to migrate, or travel seasonally between two locations or habitats. Humpback whales, one of the largest whale species, feed in the temperate seas between April and October, when food is plentiful. Then they migrate to warmer tropical waters in order to give birth and raise their young. During this breeding season, the whales do not eat at all.

Other animals spend their summers in polar seas and migrate to temperate oceans in the winter. Right whales feed in the waters around Antarctica in summer, then they head to sheltered bays around Australia, New Zealand, Argentina, and South Africa to breed. Some creatures, like herring, move inland to avoid the cold winter weather. They swim in huge numbers from ocean waters up into the fjords of Norway in the autumn.

Seaweed Forests Seaweed forests are a type of highly productive habitat specific to temperate seas. Since seaweed needs shallow waters in order to photosynthesize and solid substrate to anchor to, these plants are mostly found along rocky shores. Their ability to anchor themselves firmly there gives them a unique advantage. The same waves that make life so difficult along coastlines not only keep the seaweeds wet but also wash in nutrients for the creatures that live among these plants.

The more than 10,000 different species of seaweeds can be divided into three major groups: green algae, red algae, and brown algae. Red algae are the most numerous in ocean waters. Many of these are small plants that line rock pools along the coasts.

A frogfish camouflages itself among brown seaweed called sargassum.

The brown seaweeds include the 100 or so species of kelp, which create dense forests that are the center of activity for much coastal animal life. The giant kelp is the largest species and can grow 330 feet (100 m) long. Gas-filled bladders spaced along the fronds, or leaves, of these large seaweeds keep them afloat in the swirling ocean waters. These bladders hold the fronds near the surface, where they can be exposed to the most light. Kelp forests can only grow where there are predators for the many creatures, such as sea urchins and amphipods, that like to graze on the large fronds. The forests also serve to hide schools of fish, sea lions, harbor seals, and other creatures from predators.

The Seabed Shallow coastal waters are not the only active regions in temperate seas. The endless supply of nutrients and debris washed from the continents onto the continental shelf and the dead matter from plankton blooms and coastal habitats all eventually settle down to the ocean floor as it slopes. Every possible inch of the cliffs along the continental slope is colonized by urchins, barnacles, starfish, sea slugs, snails, amphipods, brittlestars, and many other creatures that take in the large food supply washing down from above. Sea anemones and soft corals are the most plentiful creatures in this habitat. All these invertebrates support other, more mobile sea life, like lobsters, crabs, shrimp, and fish.

As the seafloor flattens out below the cliffs beyond the continental slope, life becomes more difficult because there are few places to hide and there is less food to compete for. Some animals, like bivalve mollusks, stay buried beneath the pebbles and extend a tube that pulls in water and siphons out the small debris that it eats.

Many fish that live in this habitat have evolved flat, camouflaged bodies with upward-facing eyes and mouths. They lie on the seafloor, wait for prey to come by, then lunge for it. Other fish that live here include large species, such as Atlantic halibut, skate, and cod.

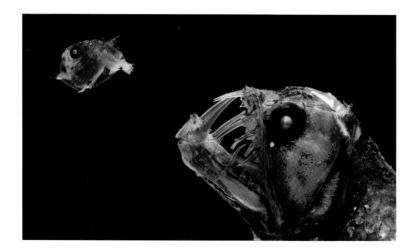

A viperfish (right) chases a hatchet-fish in the deep sea.

Polar Oceans

The Arctic Ocean surrounding the North Pole and the Southern Ocean around Antarctica are two of the smallest oceans in the world. Cold temperatures and year-round ice at the poles have strong influences on these oceans and the life in and around them. Despite the fact that parts of these regions have six months of sunlight and six months of darkness every year, they receive nearly the same amount of solar radiation annually at the equator. However, the snow and ice cover reflects 85 percent of the solar radiation that provides heat back into space. Areas without ice reflect only 5 percent of the solar radiation.

The center of the Antarctic continent is solid rock covered by a layer of ice as thick as 3 miles (5 km) in some places. This ice cap has been building for about 250,000 years, and it holds almost 70 percent of Earth's freshwater. Although the Southern Ocean is larger than the Arctic Ocean, it is warmer than the Arctic because it is connected to three other oceans. As a result, only 2.6 percent of the Southern Ocean is ice. Its waters are the roughest seas in the world because there is no large land mass to block or deflect the constant westerly winds.

The Arctic Ocean is mostly ice-covered and lies at the center of the Arctic region made up by the northern parts of the United States, Asia, and Greenland. The ice is not held together in one clump but moves around with ocean currents in huge sheets.

The polar seas go through an annual cycle of freezing and thawing, but the temperatures do not fluctuate much. The waters just barely get warm enough to melt the ice in the spring. In winter, sea ice can reach thicknesses of 3 to 6 feet (1 to 2 m). In the Arctic, 5.5 million square miles (14 million km²) of sea ice is added to the Arctic Ocean in winter. The Antarctic winter sea ice expands by 8 million square miles (22 million km²).

Life in the Cold The cold conditions in these regions surrounding the polar seas are so severe that biodiversity is very low, and some animal groups, like reptiles, are not even present here. Antarctica is one of the most barren places on Earth. Only 4 percent of the continent supports life, and it is made up mostly of small organisms, including microbes, insects, mosses, and lichens. No land mammals live there.

The movement of the ice itself also discourages life in some areas. As the sea ice is moved along by ocean currents, it crashes against the coastline, scouring any plant or animal attempting to make a home there. And the seabed isn't safe either. Icebergs—huge chunks of glacial ice floating on the ocean—can be so large and heavy that they scour the seafloor.

But, as in the temperate seas, springtime brings an explosion of growth to polar seas. When the sea ice melts, the blooms of plankton attract many migrating animals. Many rivers drain onto shallow, silty, and gravelly continental shelves in the Arctic Ocean, and active currents mix the waters. Phytoplankton can reproduce as soon as temperatures are right. In Antarctica, plankton are so active that they cover the bottom of the sea ice. Even far inland, many other creatures—including diatoms, protozoans, bacteria, fungi, and small crustaceans—thrive in meltwater channels within the ice.

The same nutrients that feed the plankton bloom also nourish the rich seabed life on the Arctic continental shelves. Crabs, starfish, and especially bivalves flourish here. Antarctic seabed life is even richer. Centuries-old sponges live in the deep waters, with corals a little higher up. Fish, starfish, crustaceans, and others thrive in shallower water. Since Antarctica broke away from the other continents so long ago, many of the creatures there are unique to this frozen land.

There is a lot of activity above the polar sea ice as well. Penguins rest, walruses raise their pups, and polar bears hunt. In the Arctic, land predators are able to increase their hunting territories when the sea ice freezes.

Animals of Antarctica Of the many different creatures in and around the Southern Ocean, probably the most important is also one of the smallest: krill. The eleven species of these tiny (2- to 3-inch/4- to 6-cm), shrimp-like crustaceans feed on the plentiful plankton in these waters. The estimated 100 to 150 million tons of krill in the Southern Ocean provide the main food source for much of the mammal life in this region, including penguins and whales.

Crabeater seals, the most abundant seal and possibly the most abundant mammal on Earth besides humans, survive mainly on krill. There may be as many as 30 million crabeater seals in the world. Although they spend most of their time in the water, they also haul themselves out onto the sea ice to rest and to breed.

The six species of whales—minke, fin, sei, blue, humpback, and right—that migrate to the Southern Ocean to feast on the bounty of krill are all baleen whales. Another species of whale, the killer whale, navigates the broken sea ice, hunting seals and penguins.

While many whale species move between two climatic regions, penguins stay within Southern Ocean waters, spending summers on the continent and migrating to sub-Antarctic islands in winter to breed. The seven species include king, Adelie, emperor, macaroni, chinstrap,

Chinstrap penguins travel across icebergs in Antarctica's Weddell Sea.

gentoo, and rockhopper penguins. Emperor penguins are the only species to spend the winter on the Antarctic continent, huddling together for warmth. They are also the largest, standing 3 feet (1 m) tall and weighing 65 to 90 pounds (30 to 40 kg).

Penguins have evolved to be flightless because they live where there are no land predators. But aquatic predators, such as leopard seals and killer whales, are plentiful, so the penguins are excellent swimmers in order to evade them.

Krill are the penguin's main food source. During the short time while krill is available the penguins breed on the snow-free shores of islands. This provides a relatively safe place to raise their young and ready access to food.

Animals of the Arctic Copepods are small crustaceans that are part of the zooplankton. They feed on phytoplankton and serve the same role in the north as krill do in the south. Most of the sea life and many bird species migrate north from southern regions in the summer to feed on the vast numbers of copepods that bloom in response to the phytoplankton.

Polar bears make full use of the winter sea ice to hunt seals. They are even able to swim considerable distances in search of food. Their fur—hollow, insulating hairs—and a thick layer of fat help keep them warm. During bitter weather, the males spend much of their time in hollowed-out pits to avoid the worst winds. Females excavate dens and spend four months in them, giving birth to their cubs after the first month. The mothers don't feed during this time and lose one-third of their body weight.

When most other Arctic animals have plenty of food to eat in the summer, polar bears have to work harder. Ringed seals, their main prey, can more easily escape into the open water in summer. If temperatures are too warm, the same insulation that shields the bears from the worst winter weather can cause them to overheat quickly, so they stay quiet and inactive during warm periods.

Though polar bears can swim in the chilly arctic waters, many walk and hunt on ice floes, which are fragments of floating ice.

A Galapagos sea lion searches for a meal in underwater caves.

3

OCEAN HABITATS

Although there are significant differences between the oceans of different climatic regions, the types of habitats and kinds of species that inhabit the oceans are common to all zones. These general habitat types include the coast, the open ocean, and the deep sea.

THE EDGE

Coastal waters represent only a small portion of the world's oceans, but they are one of the most productive ocean habitats. There are two basic types: rocky and sandy coastlines.

Sandy shores are the most common. These constantly shifting and changing environments normally achieve a natural balance between erosion and deposition: sand is washed in, sand is washed out. But coastlines do change as sand is moved from one location to another.

Temperate beach sand is usually made up of quartzite, which is a type of rock. Some tropical beaches are biological in origin, made up of eroded skeletons of marine mammals, especially coral. Rocky coasts are usually younger and the result of more violent wave action. Erosion occurs so rapidly that deposition doesn't have time to catch up with it. The steeper coastlines are battered by waves, which sometimes break the cliffs apart and wash rocks and pebbles ashore.

The opposite effect occurs in estuaries, where rivers meet the sea. Organic-rich mud from rivers washes in faster than the slow-moving ocean waves can erode it. The habitats that form as a result—mud flats and salt marshes along temperate coasts—are among the most

The estuary of the Parker River on the northeast Massachusetts coast is one of the most productive nurseries for fish, crustaceans, and other life in the United States. A great variety and number of birds both live in this area and use it as a feeding stop on their migrations.

productive coastal habitats. The calmer, salty waters here are perfect nurseries for massive numbers of fish and shellfish. Such a large food source in a relatively confined area brings in flocks of migrating birds to feast. The calmer waters also make good places to dock boats. Many shipping ports are built in estuaries. However, this industrial use often destroys valuable wildlife habitat.

Life on the Coast

As productive as these habitats are, they are very difficult places to live. The temperature, moisture, and salinity (salt content) of the water changes drastically as the tide goes in and out daily. Marine animals that inhabit sandy shores, such as clams and crabs, come out of hiding to feed on the debris that the tide washes in. When the tide is out, birds and land mammals come to feed on the exposed marine life.

Crashing waves on rocky coasts are another danger to animal life. Marine iguanas of the Galapagos Islands have strong claws that help them hang on when the waves hit. Feeding birds lift into the air when the waves come in. Seaweeds have developed holdfasts, strong appendages that anchor them to the rock.

The coast provides food for a wide variety of land and marine mammals. In different parts of the world, raccoons, bears, monkeys, beetles, and eagles come down to the shoreline to feed on washed-up plant matter, dead fish, and even dead whales.

The mix of salt and fresh water in estuaries creates a special set of problems for the creatures living there. Most estuarine animals originally came from the sea, so the fresh water is dangerous for them. Some creatures have evolved to change the fluids in their bodies to adjust for the changing levels in the surrounding waters. Salmon do this as they migrate between fresh- and salt-water environments to breed. Most estuary plants colonized these areas from land, so they have evolved ways to deal with the salt. Many secrete the salt water

Sea Turtles

Sea turtles spend most of their time alone, searching for food in tropical and subtropical waters. These long-lived, primitive creatures return to the location of their own birth every two to eight years to lay their eggs. They need the warm tropical sands to keep the eggs at the right temperature.

There are seven species of sea turtle in the world today—loggerhead, green, hawksbill, Kemp's Ridley, Olive Ridley, flat-backed, and leatherback. Loggerhead turtles are the most numerous of sea turtles. Six of the seven species are designated by the U.S. government as endangered or threatened.

Sea turtles take so long to reach maturity—fifteen to fifty years, depending upon the species—and the young are so likely to fall to predators that many may die before becoming old enough to reproduce. They are especially vulnerable to human activities like fishing, polluting, habitat destruction, and poaching. Special programs and laws have also been established to protect sea turtle eggs and the tiny hatchlings. Only with a concerted effort by many different nations will sea turtles be saved from extinction.

Newborn leatherback sea turtles must make the dangerous trek from nest to open water. In each clutch, several babies will be eaten by birds or other predators while they attempt to cross the sandy beaches.

from their leaves, while others flush their systems with enough fresh water to dilute the salt.

OUT TO SEA

The open ocean, also known as the pelagic realm, is vast. It covers 139 million square miles (361 million km²) of Earth's surface and averages 12,230 feet (3,730 m) deep. Within the top 650 feet (200 m), called the surface layer or photic zone, life-forms must stay afloat, find food, and avoid predators. The water is warm and brightly sunlit, with plenty of plankton.

Creatures have adapted one of two strategies for staying afloat—water resistance or extra fat. Plankton, for example, are wide and flat, a shape that holds them at the surface. Since fat is less dense than water, many creatures have either well-placed fat or many extra layers of it to

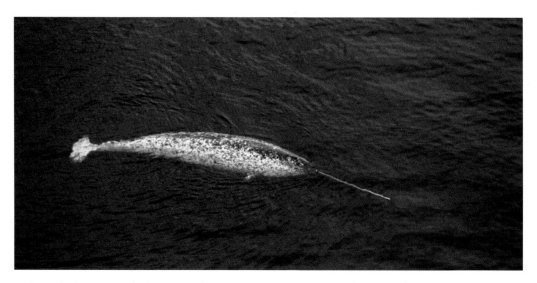

This whale, a narwhal, swims the open ocean near Canada. A male narwhal's long tusk is actually an overgrown tooth protruding from its mouth.

increase their buoyancy. Fish larvae have tiny fat droplets in their bodies, and larger creatures like whales have a lot of extra fat called blubber.

Not getting eaten is more difficult in the open water since there is no place to hide. Some fish, like mackerel for example, have light undersides and dark backs to help them avoid predators. When seen from below, their light bellies blend into the sunlit waters. From above, their dark backs make the fish difficult to see against the dark waters.

Because the biggest challenge in the open ocean is avoiding being seen by other animals, most creatures hunt and eat at night. They spend the day in lower levels of the photic zone. When night falls, one of the largest mass movements of animals on Earth occurs as an incredible number of organisms move up to the near surface layers to feed.

In the twilight zone, between 650 feet (200 m) and 3,250 feet (1,000 m) deep, water pressure increases significantly and light decreases, making life much more difficult. Since there is not enough light for photosynthesis, no plant life exists. Animals that live here depend on the small amount of food that falls from the zone above, or they prey on each other. Many are adapted to not

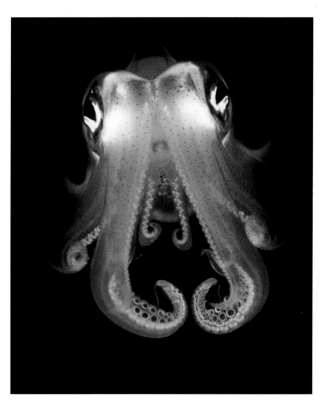

Some species of squid live far beneath the water's surface, nearly thousands of feet deep.

being seen in this low-light environment—some even have transparent bodies. Whales are one of the only creatures that can travel to the bottom of the twilight zone—which they do to hunt squid—because their large bodies enable them to tolerate the increase in water pressure.

Below the twilight zone lies the dark zone, where no sunlight penetrates. The creatures that live here are adapted to incredible water pressures a hundred times that of the surface and temperatures of a constant 34 to 37 degrees Fahrenheit (1 to 2 °C). Since there is no light, most creatures are either black or red to blend in with the dark waters. They wait for food to come to them, sensing it with receptive cells on their bodies rather than seeing it with their tiny, mostly useless eyes. But some fish use bioluminescent light that they create biochemically to attract prey, to help them see in the darkness, or to communicate.

This bioluminescent zooplankton can be found in arctic waters.

THE SEAFLOOR

Most of the seafloor, the benthic realm, is made up of a flat landscape called the abyssal plains. Small nematodes and microscopic life-forms are the most plentiful species living in the mud of the abyssal plains.Common species that hunt the seafloor are sea cucumbers, starfish, and sea urchins.

Rattail fish are the most abundant of the 1,500 or so species of fish

Life without the Sun

The constant volcanic activity that is creating the mid-ocean ridges and the rest of the seafloor makes for a harsh environment at these depths. Seawater that seeps into cracks in the ridges and is heated up by the hot rocks below the surface is forced back up into the ocean through hydrothermal vents. This extremely hot water—662 to 752 °F (350 to 400 °C)—is filled with minerals from the oceanic crust. These minerals cool down when they hit the cold seawater and crystallize to form towers called chimneys around the vents. In this environment, the lack of sunlight and the highly toxic water seem to make life impossible.

But life does exist here in dense clusters around the vents, from tubeworms to mollusks, crabs, and even fish. The tubeworms surrounding the vents are filled with a type of bacteria that uses the hydrogen sulfide that comes out of the vents and turns it into organic matter in a process similar to photosynthesis. The tubeworms feed on this organic matter and provide the bacteria with chemicals they need to live.

The northern red anemone (right) and a Scarlet Psolus sea cucumber (left) use their tentacles to grab food in the water.

that inhabit the seafloor. Some of the 200 species of ratfish, like most creatures at this depth, exist by scavenging dead plant and animal remains off the bottom, while others hunt live prey. There are also about 350 species of deep-water sharks that hunt along the seafloor.

In places, the abyssal plains are broken up by volcanoes, and the peaks of some of these break the surface of the water and become islands, like the Hawaiian Islands.

The hippopotamus is a common sight along some rivers and lakes in Africa. Its name means "river horse," and it spends much of its time cooling off in the water or eating aquatic plants.

4

RIVERS AND STREAMS

Despite the fact that less than 1 percent of all the water in the world comes from rivers, these waters are an important part of the water cycle and provide vital habitats for both aquatic and terrestrial plants and animals. Besides being a unique habitat on their own, rivers and streams provide a significant service for the many other habitats they pass through on their journey to the sea.

WATERSHEDS

Flowing waters are major shapers of land and providers of nutrients for much of the life on Earth. As with all things on this planet, water is subject to the laws of gravity. This means that wherever water comes to the surface or falls as rain, it has to flow downhill, constantly seeking its lowest level. The varied topography of the continents channels this water and the land is in turn shaped by the water's movement.

Major Rivers of the World

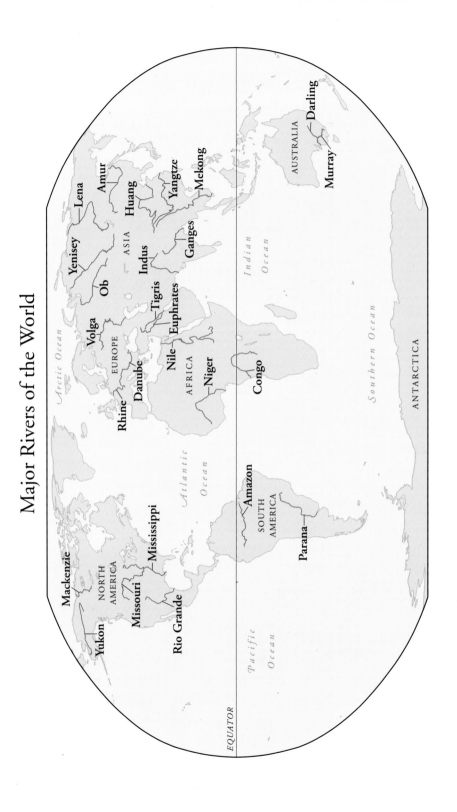

The Connecticut River begins in southern Canada and northern New Hampshire and flows south through Massachusetts and Connecticut before emptying out into Long Island Sound. Along the way, it nourishes some of the most productive farmland in the region.

Each stream that forms and flows downhill does so in its own watershed. A watershed is a portion of the landscape that funnels water into a particular stream or river. Ridgelines are usually the boundaries of watersheds. Most streams merge with other streams and then flow into rivers, which may merge with other rivers before flowing out to sea.

Watersheds can be small enough just to include individual streams or large enough to include half a continent. The Continental Divide, along the Rocky Mountains in the western United States, is the divide between the waters that drain to the Pacific on the west and those that drain to the Atlantic on the east.

Streams are classified by the number of tributaries, or feeder streams, that drain into them. River systems with streams far away from their end point tend to have the most tributaries, and the number of these decreases as the waters flow downstream. The Amazon River in South

River Patterns

Rivers are always seeking a balance, and the patterns they take are the result of those actions. Depending upon the terrain, there are three main patterns.

It is very rare that a river takes a straight course; this may occur when a stream is held in place by a steep slope along a mountain or when a river travels through very hard rock.

In areas where the load of sediment that a river carries is too large for the channel to hold, the river may break into a braided pattern of smaller channels separated by gravel or sand bars.

The most common course for a river to take is meandering, or swaying along in gentle curves. As the river rushes along its course, its force causes it to sway; the faster water is thrown against the outside of the curve. This action erodes the outer bank, while the slower water flowing against the inside bank deposits sediment picked up upstream, creating sand bars. Over time, the inside bank grows as the outside bank erodes, creating wider and wider loops. Eventually, the inside of this loop may become so narrow that the river breaks through and takes the straighter course. Sediment may build up on the ends of the cut-off loop, isolating it from the river. In this way, an oxbow lake can form.

America is Earth's largest river. The 1,000 tributaries along its 3,900-mile (6,275-km) length drain one-third of the South American continent and account for one-fifth of all the river water on Earth.

HEADWATERS

The beginning point for many streams is groundwater, the rainwater that is stored underground within aquifers. This groundwater often seeps into streams and rivers through the channels beneath them, but it can also be forced up through cracks in the rock by pressure. These springs can rise to the surface well above the elevation of the groundwater level and become headwaters, or the beginning of streams. Water also contributes to stream flow when the aquifers fill up, the soil becomes saturated, and rain flows over land in sheets. This can also be

As this glacier melts, its waters drain into Nauel Huapi National Park in Argentina. The glacial waters help to feed local rivers, lakes, and streams.

a major source of erosion. Another source of headwaters is melting glaciers. These ice caps at the peaks of mountains or covering large areas in the polar regions can be a major source of water for otherwise dry areas.

Water can flow along headwaters and down slopes very swiftly. The strong current is able to dislodge and carry with it soil and other organic debris. As it becomes wider and stronger, it can even dislodge rocks or tree roots. This in turn disrupts or changes habitats located along the rivers and streams.

FLOODPLAINS

When rivers slow down as the terrain flattens out around them, they also can widen considerably. The water slows its pace, and sediment that has been carried from upstream begins to settle out. This creates

Stream flow can vary widely throughout the year, exposing gravel and sand banks at low flow and spilling out into the floodplain during high water.

sandbars and gravel banks along the course of the river. If they aren't reshaped or eliminated by the constant water flow, plants may take root on this deposited sediment. The more plants that colonize, the more stable the land becomes, and an island may be created.

Heavy rainstorms and spring floods from snowmelt can cause these wide rivers to swell and overflow their banks onto the surrounding land. This is a natural response to the extra water that builds up every two to three years in the average river. The sediments that the waters carry away from their normal channel actually serve to replenish the soil and nutrient layer in the surrounding habitats. Many land plants can tolerate these short-duration floods, and some even come to depend on the nutrient-rich sediment the waters carry in and leave behind.

BAYS AND DELTAS

Deltas are formed when a river meets the sea. At its delta, the river slows down and creates deposits of sediment, often in a triangular shape. The name "delta" was given to these deposits because their shape resembles the fourth letter of the Greek alphabet. But deltas can actually form several different shapes, including fan-shaped or bird's-foot deltas. Although rivers generally drop 75 percent of their sediment load before

A colored satellite image shows the Mississippi River delta region in the United States.

55

reaching the sea, sediment deposited over many years by large rivers can build up large areas of land. One example of this is along the Mississippi River delta near New Orleans, where an estimated one million tons of sediment have been deposited.

An African darter catches a bream in the Okavango Delta in Botswana.

The egg-laying platypus makes its home in eastern Australia's lakes, rivers, and streams.

LIFE IN RIVERS AND STREAMS

Along the course of rivers, the interaction of water with the riverbed creates different environments. Springs, the source of many rivers, provide a clear source of water for many organisms, including semi-aquatic plants, insect larvae, beetles, and salamanders. These creatures bring land animals like minks and raccoons in from the surrounding habitats.

As the water picks up speed over the rocks and becomes a stream, oxygen, carbon dioxide, and nutrients mix in with the water. This is the richest freshwater habitat. The exposed rocks and soil and small pools provide many different niches for plants and animals to populate. More plant life, in the form of algae, mosses, liverworts, and sedges, takes hold along the edges and on rocks in the streambed. Many more insects and insect larvae populate these waters, and as a result, fish like trout can move in. The bed of the stream provides a home for many creatures as well. Mollusks and insect larvae hold on, pulling in organic debris as it passes by.

Plants like liverwort need very moist environments in order to thrive.

A pair of rainbow trout swim through stream currents.

Riffles often form where the river flows over rocky areas with still pools upstream and downstream. Stream flow can vary widely throughout the year, exposing gravel and sand banks at low flow and spilling out into the floodplain during high water. The riffles provide essential environments for feeding and breeding. The friction of the water flowing over the rocks ceates a thin layer of water about 0.1 inch (0.25 cm) thick exists on the surface of the rocks. Some creatures spend at least part of

~~~~~~

A Life in Three Worlds

Among the most interesting but often overlooked creatures living in streams are members of the insect world. There are more than 1,000 species of black flies on Earth. They are most familiar in their adult stage, nagging and biting people to get a blood meal.

They lay their eggs in swiftly flowing streams, and these hatch into larvae 0.2 inches (0.5 cm) long. This stage of their existence is spent anchored to rocks with silk threads, saliva, and tiny hooks. The larvae look nothing like the adults they will grow into—they are tubular in shape, with two sets of fanlike hairs on either side of their heads. These hairs serve to sift food from the water as it passes by.

After a few weeks, the black fly larvae enter their pupal stage by spinning a silk case inside which they will transform into adults. When they are nearly ready to emerge, gas bubbles form inside the casing and attach to the flies' body hairs. Once the casings break open, these air bubbles carry the winged adults to the surface. The black fly then flies away to spend its adulthood on land and in air.

their lives here feeding on the attached algae. Stoneflies and mayflies have flattened bodies that allow them to stay within that narrow zone, while other insects have body parts that can grab onto the rock.

There is a wide variety of fish in streams. Sculpers and darters stay near the bottom. Salmon and trout come to riffles to spawn. Trout are streamlined, fast swimmers that can move through swift currents, but they tire easily. Pools and small eddies behind rocks or islands offer quiet spots out of the direct current where fish can rest. Most fish lay their eggs on stream bottoms to avoid the strong current.

Much of the food that nourishes river systems comes from the nearby land. Leaves, stems, flowers, and fruits of trees and other plants that fall into the water are carried downstream or settle to the bottom. Bacteria and fungi begin to break this organic matter down. Insect larvae and nymphs feed on it as well. Many small dead insects, snails, and other creatures add to this debris, called drift, and provide food for many other life-forms along the river's course.

When streams widen into riverbeds, their waters are filled with sediment. The force of the current and fluctuating water levels make it difficult for much life to colonize the banks. Even in low water, if plants try to take hold, they are usually swept away after the next rainstorm. These areas of shifting and moving sediments have the lowest diversity of any flowing-water habitat.

Bald cypress trees thrive in and along lakes and swamps in the southern sections of the United States.

5

LAKES AND PONDS

Rivers have a long history of draining and shaping the landscape over millions of years. But lakes and ponds have a limited lifespan—hundreds or thousands of years at the most. Since they act as reservoirs, they hold water, living plant matter, and debris from the surrounding landscape. Over the years, the solid debris replaces the water, and the lake evolves into a swamp, then a meadow, and eventually a forest may stand where water once was. Lakes created by meandering rivers will eventually dry up, replaced by a rich plant growth that thrives on the nutrient-rich river sediment.

THE LIFE CYCLE OF STANDING WATER

Lakes and ponds are the result of Earth's varied topography. Since water always seeks its lowest level, almost all the basins and depressions that were created by landslides, erosion, earthquakes, volcanoes, glaciers, meteor impacts, animals, and humans will eventually fill with water.

Oregon's Crater Lake was formed when Mount Mazama erupted and collapsed about 7,000 years ago. This 6-mile-wide lake is part of Crater Lake National Park, one of the oldest national parks in the United States.

Deeper lakes that lie within steep valleys created by earthquakes tend to have little plant and animal life. Lakes created by glaciers tend to be shallow and have more plant and animal life. Glacial forces have created more lakes than any other geological force. As the ice sheets scraped over the land, they scoured out many basins by picking up soil and rocks and moving it to other locations, creating hills. Some of these hills and other glacial landforms acted as natural dams, holding water back as it filled the basin. Glaciers were responsible for carving out the landscape that allowed the Great Lakes of North America to form.

Lakes can be connected to streams or to underground water supplies.

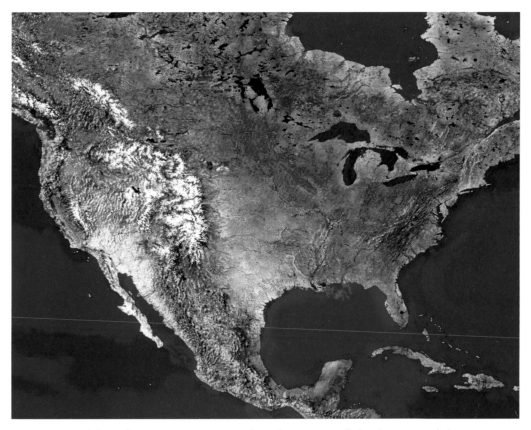

Here is a quick and easy way to remember the names of the five great lakes:
HOMES. *Each letter of the word is the first letter of the name of one of the lakes—*
Huron, Ontario, Michigan, Erie, and Superior.

Sometimes these water sources can be feeders for the lake, or they may serve to drain it, or both may apply. But as long as the input of water exceeds the output, the lake or pond will sustain itself.

However, all standing water bodies have a limited life. The process of eutrophication, the enrichment and eventual transformation of a pond or lake to a bog or swamp, is inevitable. The life of a pond or lake can be broken down into three stages: oligotrophy, mesotrophy, and eutrophy.

There is very little plant and animal life in the early, oligotrophic stage. The waters are clear and rich in dissolved oxygen. In the mesotrophic stage, sediment and nutrients have flowed in and accumulated at the bottom. Organic debris from land plants and animals have also collected. Bacteria and insect larvae feed on this rich food source. Some of the nutrients also become mixed with the upper layers of water, promoting a rich growth of phytoplankton.

In the eutrophic stage, more life has taken hold. Plant growth is dense along the pond's edges, phytoplankton activity increases, and a thick, rich, organic bottom layer forms that supports a great variety of creatures.

A eutrophic pond in Pennsylvania is filled with water plants and algae.

Eventually, all this activity consumes more oxygen than can be replaced into the system. Hydrogen sulfide, which poisons the system, is released by certain bacteria feeding on the organic debris. Many creatures die and are replaced by other species. These organisms are more tolerant of warmer, shallower, oxygen-poor environments. The lake fills in with plant matter and soil because there are fewer creatures to process the accumulating debris and sediments. Land plants can more easily take root, and this accelerates eutrophication. Eventually, a mat of vegetation floats on the water, filled with plants that can tolerate the harsh environment.

In the final stages, vegetation colonizes the water completely as it builds up its own soil layer. Shrubs and trees take hold, and eventually a forest stands in place of the water. This whole process is very slow—sediments fill in only a fraction of an inch a year. However, tropical lakes age more quickly than temperate ones because climatic conditions accelerate the process.

The aging of a water body can also be accelerated artificially. Fertilizers, sewage, or animal wastes from farms and factories may add more concentrated nutrients to lakes and ponds, which causes eutrophication to speed up.

LIFE IN PONDS

Because ponds are smaller and shallower bodies of water than lakes, life in ponds is more strongly influenced by the surrounding climate. Pond water responds more quickly to temperature variations and therefore changes significantly during the day.

The shoreline is generally ringed with plants tolerant of wet soils, such as ferns, mosses, and grasses. The roots of plants along the pond edge are often submerged. These plants include sedges, shrubs, cattails, and some herbaceous plants. As the water deepens, water lilies,

Certain plants thrive along the wet banks of ponds. These plants provide homes and food for many land and water animals.

lotuses, and other plants are able to root themselves in the pond bed and send shoots upward, where their wide, flat leaves float on the surface. Beyond this water depth, plants still grow but they are totally aquatic—they stay completely underwater. These plant zones slowly change as the nature of the pond changes by the buildup of organic matter.

The invertebrates that live in ponds are similar to some ocean creatures because they came from the ocean millions of years ago. Water striders—light enough to scurry along the surface—mosquito larvae, and other insects inhabit the top layer of water. These surface-living invertebrates often provide meals for fish, amphibians, birds, and other animals living near the ponds.

Pond water provides an ample supply of aquatic plants and insects for ducks and other birds.

Some ponds appear and disappear every year. In the early, wet spring, small shallow depressions fill with rainwater for several weeks and then dry up again during the hot days of summer. But in this short period, many creatures are able to take advantage of this vital resource. Salamanders, frogs, and some insects breed here because these small pools are free of fish and other aquatic predators. If they lay their eggs here, there is a greater chance of their young surviving.

LIFE IN LAKES

As in oceans, the life cycle of most lakes begins with phytoplankton, which rely on minerals from the surrounding rock to survive. Lakes with beds of hard rock are less productive because this rock doesn't

Beavers: Wetland Engineers

Beavers actually create their own aquatic habitats, turning streams into ponds. These amazing engineers cut down trees with their teeth and move them to the stream's outlet. They build elaborate and incredibly strong dams that block stream channels. The water then floods the area behind the dam, making a shallow pond.

The vegetation that grows along pond edges nourishes the beavers, while the lodges they build of cut trees, branches, and mud offer solid protection from predators both above and below the water. But these masters of dam engineering often come into competition with humans who don't want to see their land and roads flooded.

A beaver dam crosses part of a creek in the Alaskan wilderness.

Despite their name, river otters live in lakes, ponds, and marshes, as well as along rivers and streams. The waterways supply the otters with food such as fish, frogs, and small crustaceans.

break down easily to provide minerals. Waters with beds of glacial deposits or sedimentary rocks support more life because the minerals in this softer rock dissolve more easily. The most common lake phytoplankton are blue-green and green algae.

The top layer of a lake is where all the food is made. The algae blooms are greatest in the spring and autumn, when the mixing of waters brings nutrients to the surface, just like in the oceans. Zooplankton feed on the phytoplankton and larger, swimming creatures like fish feed on the zooplankton. In some temperate lakes, otters are the last link in the food cycle, feeding on fish, shellfish, and small mammals. In tropical rivers, crocodiles, alligators, or caimans fill this niche.

Fungi, bacteria, worms, and other invertebrates feed on the decaying organic matter at the bottom of lakes. Some fish move between the layers seasonally, feeding on zooplankton and small fish near the surface in summer, then feeding on the bottom-dwelling creatures in winter.

CONCLUSION

WATER, WATER, EVERYWHERE . . .

Creating dams to hold reservoirs for drinking water or channeling rivers to improve navigation for ships may help humans in the short term. But the consequences of this type of extreme habitat alteration are severe. Dams bury floodplain habitats beneath millions of cubic feet of water, and they also change the seasonal flow of rivers. Water levels and temperatures are altered, affecting some species' survival. Sediments that would otherwise replenish sandbars and near-shore ocean habitats are trapped. Creating straight canals removes the natural, habitat-rich flow that occurs when water moves along a meandering streambed.

Waterways are even impacted indirectly by seemingly unrelated actions. When a forest is clear-cut, sediments that had formerly been held in place by the roots of trees and surrounding vegetation suddenly flow downhill during rains and into streams and rivers. All these extra sediments cloud the waters, reducing the amount of sunlight aquatic plants can use for growth. When clear-cutting occurs along streams, the area is opened to much more sunlight, which raises the water's temperature, killing fish and other creatures that are adapted to colder waters.

Deforestation can destroy local waterways and the habitats around them. Because there are no more trees to hold the soil in place, erosion has become a serious problem in the landscape surrounding this river in Madagascar.

One of the most serious consequences of industrial pollution is the effect of acid rain on the environment. When rain forms in clouds, water vapor condenses around particles, some of these are naturally occurring, such as dust or pollen. But it can also condense around particulates of pollution, such as sulfur dioxide and nitrogen oxide. Over time, this contaminated rainwater can kill trees and poison waterways.

Even more globally significant are the impacts of global warming on the world's oceans and thus on the world's climate. Researchers have been following the increased flow from Russian rivers into the Arctic Basin. They believe this change is at least partly due to the thawing of the permafrost. This thawing produces more fresh water that floods into the ocean, which could mean a major shift in worldwide ocean circulation, and therefore a change in global climate.

Conservation measures such as organic farming (which uses no pesticides or herbicides), using sustainable forestry practices (which ensures continued growth of trees while minimizing impacts on wildlife, soils, and water bodies), legislating for controls on industrial pollution, restricting commercial fishing, and investing in research on cleaner fuels can help improve water quality.

Understanding and protecting our waterways will help to ensure a healthy future for all organisms on the planet.

Being more aware of where water comes from can make people more aware of their connection to other life-forms, the importance of the water cycle, and most of all, the importance of clean and naturally flowing water to every single organism on the planet. Decades of scientific exploration, even with modern technology, has still only revealed a fraction of what the oceans can tell humanity. It's important to learn as much as we can about these complex ecosystems and how they affect the world before any more harm comes to them.

GLOSSARY

anadromous—Fish that migrate from salt water to fresh water in order to breed.

aquifer—A layer of sand, rock, or gravel that is able to absorb water.

atoll—A coral island made up of coral reefs that surround a lagoon.

benthic realm—The seafloor.

bioluminescence—Production or emission of light from a living organism.

biota—The animals and plants of a given region.

catadromous—Fish that migrate from fresh water to salt water in order to breed.

erosion—The process of wearing away—often by natural forces such as weather and water.

estuary—A body or passage of water where a tide meets a river current or where the sea meets the end of a river.

eutrophication—The process by which a pond or lake becomes a bog or a swamp.

gyres—Circular ocean currents.

hard water—Water that contains minerals.

herbivore—Organism that feeds on plants.

mesotrophic—Lakes or reservoirs with moderate amounts of dissolved nutrients; a middle stage of a lake's aging process.

neap tides—Extreme low tides that occur when the Moon is at right angles to the Sun and Earth.

nematode—An elongated worm that may live in water or soil.

oligotrophic—Waters, such as lakes or reservoirs, with few nutrients and little photosynthetic activity; an early stage of a lake's aging process.

pelagic realm—The open ocean.

photic zone—The top 650 feet (200 m) of the open ocean.

photosynthesis—The process in green plants and other life forms of producing carbohydrates, or sugars, from carbon dioxide and water, using sunlight as the energy source.

phytoplankton—Microscopic photosynthesizing organisms that float with the water currents.

riffles—Shallow, rocky portions of a stream or river.

sediment—Soils that are deposited by wind, water, or glacial movement.

soft water—Water that contains few minerals.

spring tides—Extreme high tides that occur during full or new moons.

symbiosis—A cooperative relationship between two organisms.

thermocline—A region in water that separates the warmer, oxygen-rich surface water from cold, oxygen-poor deep water. Temperature in a thermocline decreases as depth increases.

watershed—A portion of a landscape that funnels water into a river or stream.

zooplankton—Microscopic animals or protoctists that move with the water currents; also called animal plankton.

FIND OUT MORE

Books

Byatt, Andrew, Alastair Fothergill, and Martha Holmes. *The Blue Planet: Seas of Life.* New York: DK Publishing, Inc., 2001.

Castner, James. *River Life.* New York: Benchmark Books, 2002.

Gallant, Roy. *Water: Our Precious Resource.* New York: Benchmark Books, 2003.

Web Sites

The National Oceanographic and Atmospheric Agency's (NOAA) Ocean Explorer:
http://oceanexplorer.noaa.gov
The National Marine Fisheries Service:
http://www.nmfs.noaa.gov/prot_res/index.html
Aquarius, the World's Only Undersea Laboratory:
http://www.uncw.edu/aquarius
American Rivers:
http://www.americanrivers.org

BIBLIOGRAPHY

Byatt, Andrew, Alastair Fothergill, and Martha Holmes. *The Blue Planet: Seas of Life.* New York: DK Publishing, Inc., 2001.

Caduto, Michael J. *Pond and Brook: A Guide to Nature In Freshwater Environments.* Hanover, NH: University Press of New England, 1990.

The Caribbean Conservation Corporation and Sea Turtle Survival League. "Information on Sea Turtles and Threats to Their Survival." http://www.cccturtle.org/contents.htm

National Oceanic and Atmospheric Administration. "Then and Now: The HMS Challenger Expedition and the 'Mountains in the Sea' Expedition." http://oceanexplorer.noaa.gov/explorations/03mountains/background/challenger/challenger.html

National Oceanic and Atmospheric Administration, National Marine Fisheries Service. "Sea Turtle Protection and Conservation." http://www.nmfs.noaa.gov/prot_res/PR3/Turtles/turtles.html

Pringle, Laurence. *Rivers and Lakes.* Alexandria, VA: Time-Life Books, 1985.

Robinson, James V. "Black flies or buffalo gnats (Family Simuliidae)." Texas Agricultural Extension Service, Texas A&M University. http://entowww.tamu.edu/extension/bulletins/uc/uc-019.html

Stevenson, Robert E. and Frank H. Talbot, eds. *The Illustrated History of the Earth: Islands.* Emmaus, PA: Rodale Press, 1994.

Sturm, Matthew, Donald K. Perovich, and Mark C. Serreze. "Meltdown in the North." Scientific American, October 2003; pp.60-67.

Thorne-Miller, Boyce and John Catena. *The Living Ocean: Understanding and Protecting Marine Biodiversity.* Washington, D.C.: Island Press, 1991.

United States Environmental Protection Agency. "Clean Air Markets - Environmental Issues: Acid Rain." http://www.epa.gov/airmarkets/acidrain/

INDEX

Tom Warhol is a photographer, writer, and naturalist from Massachusetts, where he lives with his wife, their dog, and two cats. Tom holds both a BFA in photography and an MS in forest ecology. Tom has worked for conservation groups such as The Nature Conservancy, managing nature preserves, and The American Chestnut Foundation, helping to grow blight-resistant American chestnut trees. He currently works for the Massachusetts Riverways Program, helping to protect and restore rivers. He has also volunteered for the Vermont Raptor Center, caring for sick, injured, and resident hawks, eagles, and owls. In addition to the Earth's Biomes series, Tom has authored books for Marshall Cavendish Benchmark's AnimalWays series, including *Hawks* and *Eagles*. He also writes for newspapers such as the *Boston Globe*. His landscape, nature, and wildlife photographs can be seen in exhibitions, in publications, and on his Web site, www.tomwarhol.com.